THOUGHT CATALOG BOOKS

How To Be A 20-Something

How To Be A 20-Something

THOUGHT CATALOG

THOUGHT CATALOG BOOKS

Brooklyn, NY

THOUGHT CATALOG BOOKS

Copyright © 2016 by The Thought & Expression Co.

All rights reserved. Published by Thought Catalog Books, a division of The Thought & Expression Co., Williamsburg, Brooklyn. Founded in 2010, Thought Catalog is a website and imprint dedicated to your ideas and stories. We publish fiction and non-fiction from emerging and established writers across all genres. For general information and submissions: manuscripts@thoughtcatalog.com.

Second edition, 2016

ISBN 978-1532775284

10 9 8 7 6 5 4 3 2 1

Cover photography by © Noah Kalina

Contents

Introduction

Brandon Scott Gorrell and Stephanie Georgopolus

We go to happy hour every day after work — does this mean we're alcoholics, or just frugal? We spend way too much time online — are we wasting our lives away, or being social the only way we know how? Are we destined to be involved with the wrong people until the end of time, or just until the end of our 20s? Does anyone have a Xanax?

Unlike the ironclad instructions provided to the generations that preceded us, the answers to our questions are as vague as our love lives, our friendships, How To Be A 20-Something and our understanding of Roth IRAs. (Really though, what is a Roth IRA?) No, the answer is not simply to marry, pop out some kids, find a stable job where we can take up space for the next 40 years, and retire. Even if we could, the world doesn't work that way anymore. Or does it? Seriously, we're asking.

It's a strange time, our 20s. It comes with a shiny exterior — but beneath it, a sense of transition and groundlessness. An impermanence informs our relationships, our jobs, our interests. It wasn't so long ago that people were ready to commit, to head to an office every morning, to discontinue casual drug use. Those people were our parents. Does the Responsible Person Gene skip a generation, or…?

Despite all the confusion and self-doubt, there's something amazing about this grace period before 'real life' begins — before we get a car, a career, and a registry at Bed Bath & Beyond. It's liberating to be allowed to experiment with lovers, careers, and identities. It's empowering to know that we're the next generation. It's exciting to be tied down to no one, to nothing (well, other than loan debt). Obligations are oppressive. Irresponsibility is freedom. Loving someone truly for the first time is unforgettable. Our 20s are romantic — even if our love lives aren't.

In *How To Be A 20-Something*, a compilation of articles originally published at ThoughtCatalog.com, we tried to capture some of the key characteristics of the rollercoaster the 20-something generation is riding. Megan Boyle illustrates just how void of traditional romance our hookups have become in her essay, "A Guide To Vague Relationships," which advises us to avoid the word "girlfriend" and look into acquiring a small pet to ward off the loneliness synonymous with long-term booty calls. In "How To Have Sex With Me One Time" by Sarah Nicole Prickett, we're instructed how to pull off the elusive one-night stand with grace. And in "Notes On Dating A Crazy Girl," Oliver Miller explores what can happen when you date a bona fide Girl, Interrupted.

But being in your 20s isn't all about the pursuit of a warm body to sleep next to. In "For Immediate Release: Recent College Grad Discovers She Chose The Wrong Major" by Stephanie Georgopulos, a 20-something just out of college realizes the education she went heavily into debt for may not end up paying off (unless half-bottles of red wine pay the rent). "Funny Drug Story" by Giancarlo DiTrapano is an account of a MDMA trip gone hilariously wrong. And in "Don't Wake Up Alone On A Saturday Morning," Ryan O'Connell writes about waking up one day and realizing that your friends have moved on without you. (#dark.)

We don't want this compilation to paint a pretty picture of our generation. But we don't want to paint an ugly one, either. Life, at any age, is not either/or. Nor is it black and white. It's Fifty Shades Of Grey! It's a series of highs, lows, and everything in between. A decade yet to have been narrowed down by the experience, clear preferences, and habits that define us as we get older. That's what we wanted to illustrate with this collection: that being in your 20s sucks, but also, it's awesome. And *How To Be A 20-Something* celebrates this dichotomy the best way we know how — with wine, Ambien, and way too much self-reflection.

1

Why Being In Your 20s Is Awesome

Ryan O'Connell

Being in your twenties is all about discovering which things hurt you and what makes you feel good. You go in blindly, practically pricking yourself with a dull blade, and then you walk out with tougher skin. One day you'll stop pricking yourself altogether. Maybe. I don't know. How would I? I'm just a twentysomething, remember?

This is what your twenties are for – to feel and see as much as you can, to take advantage of not being tied down to anything and anyone and to go balls to the wall with everything that you do. You're a raw nerve. You hate getting upset over little things, about being constantly unraveled by ignored text messages, parents, grades, and friends, but you have to remember something: you don't know yourself entirely yet. Before the age of 20, you were mostly under your parents care, a reflection of what was going on around you. You didn't have the option to make your own choices. You were merely living the life someone set out for you. Being in your twenties allows you to start carving out the life you want for yourself. Everything is on your terms now which seems daunting but is actually liberating. For the first time in your life you're the boss.

It's important to talk about why your twenties are great because it seems like we spend so much of our time wanting to be somewhere else other than where we are. Think about it. Why the hell are we in such a hurry to live some boring grown up adult life that we saw at a Crate & Barrel? Because once we do get there, we're stuck for a long time. The novelty's going to wear off, we're going to get married and have babies, and everything will be amazing but don't think for a second that you won't be nostalgic for this time. Don't think for a second that you're not going to miss those nights you spent putting on your make up, changing five million times, drinking wine, smoking cigarettes out your apartment window, and going to some silly party, a party that feels like all the others you've been to but still has the right to feel special. You will miss all of this. This is a luxury. It's going to leave us eventually so you better freaking enjoy it. You better enjoy every lame ass party, every awkward kiss, every 5 AM hangover, every drug experience, every crappy apartment, because one day it will all be gone and you'll just be left with the pictures and the bruises and nothing else. Youth is fu**ing magic. Don't you get it? Look at your skin! Touch it. Look at your smooth legs and stomach. Grab it. When you're older, you'll want all of this again so bad. You'll possibly spend so much money to get some semblance of it back. Now it's yours for free.

We're not stuck. Even if it feels like we are, it's not true. We're the opposite of stuck. As twentysomethings, we're constantly moving — apartments, relationship, cities, jobs. Anything is possible. People are ready for you. They want to hear what you have to say. They look at you and are curious about what words are going to come out of your mouth. You're the new generation. What do you have to say? Don't bite your tongue. One day you'll be pushed aside for a younger "fresher" perspective so you better get it out now. Make a mark. Make a stain. Make something.

Remember the fear, remember the promise, remember the nights you wanted to curl up in a ball, remember the people you're not supposed to remember, remember not knowing yourself, remember the moment you started to feel safe and like this life you're leading is really yours. You're going to be scared, you're going to bruise your knees and not know how they got there, you're going to try to fruitlessly forge a connection with someone who won't ever get it, you're going to lose the person that means the most to you and find your way back to them. You're going to be a twentysomething because that's what you are and all you know how to be. You should love every single moment of this hot mess of a decade. Chances are you'll miss it before you even get to say "I'm 30."

2

For Immediate Release: Recent College Grad Discovers She Chose The Wrong Major

Stephanie Georgopolus

FOR IMMEDIATE RELEASE

August 2nd, 2011
Contact: Stephanie Georgopulos, Flack
Stephanie@ThoughtCatalog.com

PRESS RELEASE

RECENT COLLEGE GRAD DISCOVERS SHE CHOSE THE
WRONG MAJOR

*Public Relations industry discovered to not be the cesspool of
parties and swag bags promised, who would've thought?*

NEW YORK, NY – She remembers her first NYC party – the
sequins, the liquor sponsor no one's ever heard of, and best
of all? The gift bags. "I went to the head of the Mass Comm

department the next day and declared a major," a recent college grad remembers. But she soon found that landing the title of Public Relations Junior Account Executive wasn't all the glitz and glam she'd been promised.

"My job sucks," the recent college grad declares. "If I knew I was going to have to spend the entire day begging other people to care about my client – who *I* don't even give a crap about? I would've majored in something else. *Anything* else."

The recent college grad likens PR to begging your parents for a raise in your allowance or pleading with a professor for a better grade. "It's like, hey, I know I don't deserve what I'm asking for, in all reality I'm pitching you a crap product and you'll get nothing out of helping me besides some almost-expired samples of organic foot paste, but I really need this – if I'm ever going to make it out of the woods and represent a client that isn't based in New Jersey, *I need this write up.* Please. *Please,*" the recent college grad reports. "It's pathetic."

"I have other friends in PR, and they're just as miserable," she says. "One works seventeen hours a day – *seventeen hours a day.* If your client needs seventeen hours of PR a day, they're in the wrong business." The grad takes six Advil and continues, "Another is in pharmaceuticals. You'd think she'd at least be able to swipe some samples for the rest of us, to help us *deal*, but only the Upper Levels have access."

While the recent college grad feels remorseful for her chosen path, she remains optimistic. "You know, it's not always bad. Once I got to take home half a bottle of wine that was leftover from a client showcase we did. Sure, it was red, and I don't really drink that, but it's a start. Someday, I imagine I'll take home an entire bottle. Can you mention that I'm looking for work? I have a degree, experience with a top NYC PR firm, and I own two Hervé Léger bandage dresses."

The recent college grad is looking for a new job in related fields and owns two Hervé Léger bandage dresses.

3

An Email To Our Parents

Brandon Scott Gorrell

Dear our parents,

Hi parents. How are you? We hope you're doing good. It was nice to see you over this year's holidays. We love home cooking. We were thrilled to hear that you still think we're great, that you're proud of us "no matter what," that you think we'll get what we want because you know that when we put our mind to something, we can do anything. We hope you continue to feel that way.

We know that we're not making much money, and that this might disappoint you, despite the fact that you'd never say it. We know that you know that when we say we're freelancers, it really just means we're mostly unemployed. That when we say we have an internship, it really just means we're groveling at someone's feet for an imaginary job where the pay is half in real estate advice and half in a number of "connections" who will open doors for more promising internships. Internships that pay $500 stipends after a 20-hour a week six month "trial period." And we know this wasn't what you were expecting. And we're writing, among other reasons, to say sorry for that.

We're also writing to say sorry that we've been completely and shamefully reckless with Facebook and Twitter over the past couple of years. We're sorry that we let you discover these completely new and strange sides of us that we were developing this whole time without your knowledge. We're sorry you had to get this information from the internet, rather than directly from us. Please don't take it personally. It just somehow felt like the entire internet understood our problems more than you. Or maybe it wasn't even like that. We can't explain it.

We hope we haven't hurt you. And we know we usually don't write long letters like this – we're really consumed with ourselves – and that you'd rather talk about this face-to-face, but it's just more comfortable over email. It always has been.

Anyways, we have some questions. We guess we'll start when we were born. It was in the late 1980s and we lived in the suburbs, and you were in your 20s. Can you remind us again why you were in your 20s? Why did you decide to have us then? Because we're in our 20s now and when we think of 'owning' a child, we also think 'no.' It wouldn't make any sense – we have things to do. People with whom to have sex. Drugs to consume. Countries to travel. Existential crises to drive us into depression. A job that pays over $20,000 a year with benefits to find. Expectations to realize unrealistic.

Which leads us to our next question. How did you guys have

enough money to raise us? To eat out at Bennigan's and all-you-can-eat buffets and Pizza Hut and Marie Calendars and variously-named steakhouses on a weekly basis? To buy a car? To go to freaking Disneyland. We mean – we're pretty capable individuals. No offense, but it seems like we're even much more savvy than you – that our skill sets are so much more relevant in today's world. But we're unemployed or baristas or dog walkers. We're making like $10 an hour.

We really wonder what you think of us now. You with your things called Pensions and Retirement Plans and 401Ks. These things that guarantee you money for the rest of your life. The retirement homes you've already purchased in Florida. The boats you have to go with them. The gated communities in Washington State. Every suburban mansion with central heating and a view of the ocean in San Diego. A dog. A barbecue. Furniture bought new. Basic medical insurance.

We don't mean to harp on you. We don't mean to imply anything negative about you. We love you. Your lives just seem really foreign. You work at the offices of companies that sell logistics technology, that sell the component parts of golf clubs, that sell mortgages. Totally esoteric companies that seem at a vast distance of abstraction from our day-to-day lives that we have no idea how they're worth any money at all.

We should get together soon. Maybe you can come to our cities. You probably can't stay at our place (would be sort of cramped) and you'd have to get a hotel, but we want you to tell us how to do what you're doing. Getting all that money. Don't tell us that it's okay that we have no prospects – that we're just living the "minimal" lifestyle. Don't say that you're like us; that you know how to live the "minimal" lifestyle too. You have a freaking car.

But that's okay. We're definitely not vindictive about your success. We only thought it would be different when we grew up and we're worried that we haven't met your expectations. We have this feeling of dread about the future, this feeling that our world's not going to turn out like yours did. Can you help at all?

How's next month? Or Mother's Day? Call us.

Love you,
Us

4

Notes On Dating A Crazy Girl

Oliver Miller

No one ever sets out to date a crazy girl, in the same way that no one ever sets out to become a member of a cult. No one's like, "HEY MAYBE I'LL JOIN AN INSANE CULT TODAY." No, you just gradually get sucked in – step by step, day by day, hour by hour – until eventually, you're just as crazy as she is.

It's like Stockholm Syndrome. It's like how Patty Hearst ended up becoming a member of the Symbionese Liberation Army. Crazy people just wear you down like that. You go from "Ohmigod I can't believe these insane people kidnapped me," to "Fuck it, maybe I will help rob a bank," to, "…Wow, this machine gun fires a lot more smoothly than I thought it would!"

In retrospect, the fact that Amber had no real furniture in her apartment should have been a tip-off. She also had no TV, no internet, no decorations on the walls, etc… She said that she was a sculptor, but there were no sculptures…anywhere in the apartment. Not that I care about watching TV or even about sculpture that much, but overall, the effect was troubling. Or, the effect should have been troubling, had I been paying attention at all.

But that's how crazy girls (or guys, no doubt) end up tricking you. What later presents itself as true craziness only seems like mild quirkiness in the beginning. So she didn't have any furniture. What did I care? …How could I have predicted that two months later, Amber would be screaming at me on the phone, telling me that she could have me hunted down and killed by a team of military experts? THIS IS ACTUALLY SOMETHING THAT SHE SAID TO ME. "I could have your legs broken, if I wanted to," she said. "…Bring it on," I mumbled back. "My life couldn't get that much worse at this point. Cue the leg-breaking."

But she didn't look crazy. She didn't have dark hair or smeared mascara; she didn't wear all black or act "goth-y." She looked like what she essentially was: a rich WASP-y girl from New England.

On our first date, we got drunk at a bar. I knocked over a plate and broke it. I was comforted by the fact that she was somehow drinking more than I was, which is nearly impossible. I took a bunch of Adderall and we went back to her place and fucked four times. Then we woke up in the morning and did it again. Within a few days, I was living with her.

Look, I don't hold myself blameless here. Clearly, I am not immune from acting crazy myself. I drink too much, I smoke too much, I actually have a form of OCD which involves pulling out your own hair. No one moves in with a girl after three days, but I did. But there's a difference between being "crazy" and being *crazy crazy*.

Amber was bipolar; she had bipolar disorder. And she would drink massive amounts of booze on top of her "meds," ignoring the warning labels on her medicine bottles — the warning labels which said that drinking on top of her pills would lead to violent mood swings.

Amber was also brutal. I soon learned that anything that I said could be grist for a potential fight. Once, she started screaming at me because I said that she was "skinny."

"YOU THINK THAT THIS IS SKINNY?" she said, taking a slug from her juice glass full of vodka. "I'LL TELL YOU WHAT SKINNY IS. I USED TO BE ANOREXIC, NOW THAT WAS SKINNY."

Oh, great… I thought.

"Um, I meant it as a compliment?" I said.

"YOU DON'T KNOW WHAT YOU'RE TALKING ABOUT!!!"

———

Going for a walk, buying a TV, the proper way to cook grilled cheese — these could all be the potential causes of fights. Soon, my voice acquired a permanent quaver at the end of sentences. "Honey?" I would say. But I would say it like this: "Hon-neeeee?" As in, *please don't throw anything else at me.*

"WHO THE FUCK WERE YOU TALKING TO ON THE PHONE?"

"Honey? My friend Tiffany?"

"OHHH, TIFFANY, WHAT, ARE YOU GUYS GONNA FUCK NOW?"

"She lives 1,500 miles away. She's married. I gave her away at her wedding. How can I… fuck her?"

"I JUST CAN'T HANDLE THE LIES ANYMORE, OLIVER."

…Eeek.

But Amber was really good in bed; and there you have my epitaph, or one of them, anyway: "But she was really good in bed." It's not a good excuse for dating anyone, but I guess it's all I've got.

Being insane really helped Amber be uninhibited in bed. We would have endless loud screaming fights, and then endless loud screaming sex. "Oh, fucking pound me!" she would scream. "I'm gonna make you come all night!" Okay then.

Her orgasm noise was like the dying wail of something or

other: "OHMIGAAAAAAAAAAAAAAWWWWD." Meanwhile, our neighbors would be banging angrily on the walls of her apartment. Yes, I had become that person. I had become *the member of the couple that the neighbors hated.*

———

There were other consolations as well. Amber would tell me fifteen times a day that she loved me more than anyone else ever could; that she understood me in a way that no one else ever could. Okay then.

And she thought that every girl on the face of the earth wanted to sleep with me. Since I don't actually look like Brad Pitt in real life, this was highly flattering.

"WHO WERE YOU JUST TALKING TO?"

"…The waitress?"

"THAT BITCH BETTER WATCH OUT, I SAW HER MAKING EYES AT YOU."

"…The waitress that I just gave money to for a cheeseburger?"

And that's when it starts. You start to believe your own crazy hype. *Wow, maybe every single girl ever does want to fuck me,* you think. *Wow, when she's not screaming at me, my girlfriend just constantly tells me how amazing I am.*

———

I broke up with Amber a while ago, but I still hear from her.

She calls me up ten times a day to tell me that she loves me. Every tenth time or so, I pick up, and then, somehow, we get into a huge fight. …But in a way, this is all my fault. I know I shouldn't pick up the phone, but I do. I just like the attention, I guess.

And so, I must confess here that I find crazy people to be fun and entertaining. …And so, it's my weakness, I guess. Life with Amber was interesting; never a dull moment. Because she was crazy, she wasn't distracted by quotidian concerns the way that you or I are. Every second of her life was laser-focused on something or other. Yeah, she would scream at me for ignoring her if I dared to send my boss an email, but she also told me continually that I was the most awesome sexy genius of *ever*.

Dating a crazy girl plunges your life into a sort of lurid Technicolor format. I did it, so I know. You get good attention and you get bad attention, but you get *attention*. And now that I've broken up with Amber, my life is dull again. The lights have gone down in the theater. Everything is in lame black-and-white. It's safer here, but also more boring, and that's sad, in a way.

5

How to Have Sex With Me One Time

Sarah Nicole Prickett

Don't tell me I'm beautiful. I'm here, aren't I? Like, I'm here. I'm doing this and I have a reason…somewhere. I know you're supposed to think I'm beautiful, and I know I'm supposed to think so too, for now. Your mother probably had you believe that no girl really wants to have sex, and thus you think you have to talk her into it. You have to make her feel special. But see, I'm not your mother's daughter. At least I hope not. Gross.

And what does it mean, beautiful? I guess a lot of girls are beautiful when it's dark and their heads are all the way down there, aren't they? Aren't they all?

While you're not talking, don't ask me if I know how long you've wanted this. I don't. And don't ask me what I'm thinking. If I were thinking, there's maybe a ten percent chance I would be here. Let me for once not think about what happened before this and what will happen next. Let me be in the moment. But if there's a god, for his sake, do not say anything that includes the words "in the moment."

Tell me I have great tits. Tell me you like the smell of sweat.

These are small things that I can believe and I will believe them more if you show me, and believe me. All I want is to believe. Show me how you stroke your cock when you wake up in the morning and you have a little time. And show me how you like me and how you like me to to touch you and how much you want to touch me.

I'm saying: feed me cock. Not lies.

Because look, I won't be mad if you never text me again. I'll be mad — like crazy scorned hellcat mad — if you never text me after you, while you were getting me naked and hopefully wet, called me the best thing that's happened to you all year. I'll say, this is how you treat the best thing that's happened to you all year? I'll say, maybe my first clue should've been the word "thing." Postscript: you're a prick.

The less you promise now, the less you have to answer for later, basically; and anyway the best thing you can do with your mouth is kiss me. Everywhere. If you can kiss me and touch me at the same time: do that. Keep doing it. If you're doing it right, you'll hear me. For now, a little help: it helps if you don't touch me like you'd touch a newborn or an orchid. Please, I eat; I'm not going to break. I don't want to be handled with care. What care?

Don't try to be good in bed. You're not good in bed. We're good in bed. Right, or we're not, but let's stay positive (not that kind of positive). We're in this together. While it all happens you're just a boy and I'm just a girl and we've been doing this since we were naked in gardens in some ancient sacral text.

Relax.

If you read it in a magazine, don't do it.

If your ex-girlfriend liked it, do it.

I don't mean whip out all your kinks at once. Let's have a little mystery. Let's not do anything that could land us in emergency because, just a guess, you're not going to be in love with "the moment" when that moment is "please state your relationship to the patient" on an official form. Besides, I don't need you to be different when you're already this whole new boy in my bed. If you can't get off on just straight-up sweat-and-vanilla fucking, you should go get professional help, and I do mean that kind of pro.

As for me, I'm trying not to be a whore. I'm not doing this for love or affection or anything in exchange. I'm doing it for the only reason anyone should ever have sex, which is: I want to. All I want to feel is want. And, yes, wantedness and wantonness. All that.

Make me cum. Again: you'll know. Orgasms are like the price of heels at Balenciaga. If you have to ask, get the fuck out.

After that, and only after that, you'll cum too. I mean, I'm pretty sure you will. The odds are in your favor. Then you can collapse into me and close your eyes and breathe and if you have to, I mean if you really have to, you can say I'm beautiful and I won't say I'm not.

6

I Am Extremely Talented And Important

Brad Pike

If you knew who I was, you wouldn't so callously disregard my resume, my cover letter, my LinkedIn profile; no, you would assign me a high-paying sinecure in which I can look at YouTube all day while respectfully pretending to not be looking at YouTube all day, a job that warrants my sparkling personality and all-around likability, a job in which I can unleash my immeasurable talents at, I dunno, stuff or whatever. My mind is a seat of infinite potential that I sit on like a fat man pooping on a porta potty toilet. Five years previous experience? – that's inconsequential when faced with the endless possibilities at hand. No, I haven't done anything significant with my life, but on the other hand, I could do *anything significant* with my life. That's the magic of youth! Allow your company to drink at its wellspring of unforeseen latent talent!

Look into my eyes. Gaze into my soul. Take off my shirt. Don't you know who I am? I'm extremely talented and important, you dumb idiot.

If you would just read my blog, maybe you would understand

how great I am. It documents my myriad *intense feelings*, YouTube videos of cats, and image macros of Obama. When you watch the video of kittens playing in a Christmas tree, you will say to yourself, "He likes funny interesting things and is therefore, according to the transitive property, a funny interesting person. We must hire him at once!" You will think this because you are a shrewd employer who understands that extensive knowledge of internet memes translates directly into high levels of productivity for your company. Read the poems I've posted, the ones about my existential despair and psychological turmoil, and you will understand what a deep person I am, full of feelings, so many feelings, all explicated in complicated nuanced metaphors, with words like "lacuna," "osculate," and "turbid." You probably don't know what those words mean, but I do – my mastery of SAT words indicates I'm extremely smart. Also, important. And talented. And super cool.

A cursory glance through my Facebook will reveal a high percentage of photos of me holding a plastic red cup while making a bemused facial expression, so I might as well confirm that, yes, I am an alcoholic. But think on this for a moment: F. Scott Fitzgerald, Ernest Hemingway, William Faulkner, and Charles Bukowski were all alcoholics – what does that tell you? Huh? Put the pieces of the puzzle together, and I trust you'll form the correct conclusion (hint: I'm exactly the same as them). I mean, I haven't written a book, but I feel strongly that I *could* write a book, and if I did, it would be the best book. The language would be so rich, so lyrical, so audacious, Emily Dickinson's corpse would spontaneously reanimate, march to the nearest cyber-café, and email me a blurb to put on the back cover.

I should record everything I say and turn it into a 24/7 podcast called *Everything I Say is Interesting and Important.*

I'm worldly, and I know current events. I watch Jon Stewart every day, and sometimes people talk about the news on Twitter. One day, I'll be famous for whatever talent I've yet to manifest, and Ellen DeGeneres will interview me about politics. Then I will say something astonishingly incisive like, "America needs to tax the rich," or "Congress is full of dummies." Everyone will stand up and applaud for approximately five minutes until Ellen has to sternly command them to quiet down, but even then, they will keep clapping, and some people will be crying even, puking up blood from sheer overwhelming *consensus.*

If I could make a movie, it would have a shocking montage at the end where the main character realizes that he and the bad guy are the same person, that he actually has multiple personality disorder. It would be dramatic and surprising. Not that you asked, but my favorite director is Kubrick.

In my mind, I'm the star of a show called *My Super Awesome Life* that airs everyday, wherever I am, all the time. All these other people, these hapless nobodies, my friends, family – they're just supporting actors in the ongoing serialized story of my life, and just like with Tim Allen on *Home Improvement,* none of the other characters matter. Sometimes though, these other people think they're the stars of their own shows; someone will try and contribute to the conversation as if they're also important, but of course, it's never as funny or interesting as what I say, and they know it, and I know it, and everyone knows it, and then I must say something cruel and acerbic to make him feel like when he dies, no one will attend the funeral.

Deep down, I know my mind is a swollen spider's egg, waiting to burst open and release a million hungry babies, who will gnaw and nibble their way through my skull and stream from my eyes, nose, and mouth. I can see the breakdown approaching, the sudden realization of what I really am. My ego's stretched too thin like an overinflated hot air balloon. Something has to give.

But I've gotten really off topic. As I was saying, I'm extremely talented and important, and you should absolutely hire me because, after all, God didn't make the world for you. He only made it for me. I'm the best. Me. No one else.

7

How To Drink At Home By Yourself

Stephanie Georgopolus

Have 'one of those days.' Sit at a desk in a small room and unconsciously nash your teeth until it's too painful to continue. Hear your jaw click whenever you open your mouth too wide and mention this to people and they'll say, "It sounds like you're stressed out" and you'll think, "When is anyone not stressed out, seriously, someone answer that question." Think, "I'm going to have a drink when I get home."

When someone invites you to hang out later, to go to Happy Hour or their coworker's Birthday Drinks Thing or to their Couch To Watch *Law & Order: SVU*, respond uniformly to their requests: Wish I could, but I'm just really not up for drinking tonight. This is half of the truth; you're not up for drinking tonight *with other people*. Tonight, you drink alone.

Take the subway home and when a chubby 7-year-old accidentally puts all of his weight on your foot, resist the urge to kick him.

Go to the liquor store and spend no more than $12 on a bottle of wine. Buy Yellowtail or Barefoot or some other Native

American-inspired brand that you used to drink in college when you wanted to feel sophisticated. As the cashier swipes your debit card, wonder if it'll get declined.

When you get home, peel your clothes off and find your sweatpants. Karl Lagerfeld once said that sweatpants are a sign of defeat, so now you like to wear them whenever you've given up. Pour yourself a glass of wine and rest it on a side table and consider wearing a pair of comforting socks. See the glass of wine from the corner of your eye and channel Kirsten Cohen or some other first-world-problem-with-a-drinking-dilemma television character. Sip your wine. Release an over-exaggerated sigh. Finish your drink and refill your glass.

Once you're two deep, grab a refill and turn on the television. Watch *Law and Order: SVU*. Get indignant if it's an episode where Stabler and Benson are 'taking a break.' "Who is this bitch, even. Who is she, making out with Stabler when he's separated from Kathy. GTFO. Oh Benson, you work in computer crimes now? Since when? You don't know shit about computers. Give me a goddamn break with this crap. I love this show."

Refill your glass. Decide that you're hungry and pull up Seamless Web. Want something extremely specific that you can't have, like a Bloomin' Onion. Wonder how they even make those Bloomin' Onions that kind of look like an untreated wartime STD or something but are so damned delicious that who cares, really? Wonder if you can type 'Bloomin' Onion' into the 'Special Instructions' section of your order, if that will make one magically appear. Settle on your usual BBQ

Chicken Burrito, which is the worst thing Tex-Mex has done to your bank account, your waistline, and America. Refill your glass twice while placing your order. So Seamless.

Channel surf while waiting for your food and pick the show your roommates never let you watch more than four consecutive episodes of, like *Degrassi*. Immediately become emotionally vested in the plotline. Refill your glass. When someone dies, graduates, gets shot, loses their baby, accuses a teacher of sexual molestation, almost falls off of a roof, lies to someone they love, is confronted about their drug problem, or comes to the powerful realization that nothing will destroy their relationship with their best friend, let a single tear trickle down your face. Life is so hard.

Now you're in the mood to cry. YouTube "High and Dry" by Radiohead and close your eyes and imagine an idyllic montage of you and everyone you've ever slept with picking pumpkins and making out in cabs. Picture things that never even happened, like the time you snuck some frosting onto your lover's nose and they had no idea it was there so they just stood around looking helpless and boy that thing that never happened was so cute, wasn't it? This would make a great opening scene for a Jennifer Aniston film.

Your doorbell is ringing and you wonder if it's not The One Who Got Away coming back for you, well, one of them at least, mostly all of them got away, actually, if you want to be a stickler about it. Wipe away your *Degrassi* tears and walk to the door. "Francois," you say, "Is that you?" You don't know a Francois, but you wish a Frenchman would show up on your doorstep to validate you with his tongue and judge you for drinking cheap white wine. Alas, all that awaits you is a BBQ Chicken Burrito, which happens to smell like defeat. Good thing you wore your sweatpants.

Eat your burrito like it did something wrong to you. Poke and prod it with a fork and watch its insides spill all over the tin-foil it came in and all over the floor. Stupid burrito. Spill some rice and beans down your shirt and feel really good because no one can see you. No one knows about the burrito massacre taking place in this recliner chair right now. And no one will find out, *not no one.*

8

What 20-Somethings Want

Ryan O'Connell

You want to find someone who will pick you up from the airport. It's such a kind gesture but also one you would expect from someone who loved you a reasonable amount. The thought of having to wait for a shuttle while others are embracing their loved ones on the curb might just be too much for your little heart to bear. Where's your car full of love? Where are the people who are going to make you feel welcome in this city? And, no, you are NOT going to take a taxi. You have too many friends who like you WAY too much for you to be taking that nonsense. Right? Hello? I'M AT TERMINAL 3. WHERE ARE THE PEOPLE THAT LOVE ME? Dear god, people have started to hug on the curb. Come quick!

You want to live closer to your parents. It's not because you need to see them more. God no! Who would ever do a thing like that? It's for if you ever *wanted* to see them. If their health took a turn for the worse, god forbid, or if you ever felt lonely and needed to just sleep in a home that felt warm and loved, you could do it. Living far away from them has its advantages but you're starting to realize how much you miss out on by being on the opposite end of the country. If you lived in the same city as your parents, feeling safe and secure would just be one phone call and a twenty minute drive away.

You want to be "stable" and see yourself make real progress. You would love to find the key to adulthood (Um, I think I saw it at Crate & Barrel next to the colanders) and not want to get drunk at happy hour anymore. It's quickly turning into unhappy hour and you're trying hard not to become a casualty of your age. You want nothing more than just to make it through the twenty-something rain and land on a nice job, a nice couch that wasn't purchased from IKEA, and, most importantly, someone's nice dick and/ or vagina.

You want to develop a backbone and start saying no to having lunch with the random friend from high school. In fact, you want to abolish "catch up" lunches altogether. People are either in your life as it happens or not in it at all. Sitting through these elaborate brunches with people who once meant something to you but no longer make sense, and talking about how great your lives are going while reflecting on the good ol' days is a slow form of masochistic torture. It feels like performance art: *INSERT SMILE HERE* and *INSERT "I'M IN A REALLY GOOD PLACE. HOW ABOUT YOU?" HERE*. You've been through so many lunches like this that you could practically do them in your sleep. In fact, you should probably just arrive to the restaurant 15 minutes early and place a giant stuffed animal in the chair in place of you and run out before your old school chum arrives. Don't worry, they won't notice! You can even attach a tape recorder and have it come on intermittently to say things like, "You look great! Can I have the Egg's Benedict?" Or my personal fave catch-up topic, "I saw on Facebook that you two broke up. What happened?"

You want to know that you're not insane, that there are other 24-year-olds have never been in a relationship before, or that other people have gotten too drunk and vomited on their taxi driver before and it's all okay because this is growing up. Or something. You're not actually sure. You never received an official manual but you figure that this is what it's all about — feeling alienated and vomiting on strangers and never having as much sex as you would like. You just want to know that the things you're going through aren't unique, that other people are in the same rickety broken down palace of a boat. I mean, you don't mind being crazy so long as there are people out there who are equally as psycho. You'd prefer it if they were actually crazier than you, so you could feel good about yourself and where you're at in your life.

You want a job, a vacation, heath insurance, validation, a back rub, a scalp massage at the place where you get your haircut, people who are jealous of you, an ex who won't stop texting you when they're drunk, Twitter followers, happiness maybe sorta, someone to buy you lunch at a fancy restaurant, a mentor who can tell you what the hell to do with your life, a reliable internet connection, a reliable human connection, a gift card to the grocery store, dinner parties with friends where everyone will pretend to have their crap together for just one night, a nice flirty text message to wake up to every morning for the rest of your life, for everyone to like you even if you don't like anyone, and one of those nights that doesn't end till 9 AM and reminds you what it feels like to be young and alive. Oh, and $$$. That's all. Think you can get that for me? For us?

9

Funny Drug Story

Giancarlo DiTrapano

This one time in college, a few friends and I were in the court-yard of a bar on Decatur St. in New Orleans. We had these rolls to do. During this period in New Orleans there were these rolls that people called chocolate-chip cookies because they were white with little brown specks. They came on really strong at first and it felt like it was heavy dope or something but then it would ease up and you'd be able to move and talk and maybe dance and have the time of your life whenever, wherever you wanted. I remember people saying that the brown specks in the rolls were "heroin spots" and that sounded pretty cool at the time because none of us knew how awesome (horrible) heroin actually is (can turn out to be). We all ate the rolls, and about twenty minutes later my friend Dan (who had also just eaten a gigantic platter of ribs and fries and coleslaw and potato salad that looked disgusting and I don't even know why he ate a bunch of food when he was get-ting ready to do ecstasy because that doesn't really mix very well), he said his stomach didn't feel good. Then he grew a little white. But Dan was already really white so he turned more of a grayish-green color like pale people (gross) always do. His hue was quickly waning. Dan had long black stringy hair and a gigantic mouth that was always smiling and laughing but it also took up most of his face because it was so big. You know those people whose faces are all mouth. Dan's color and sickened demeanor made it obvious what was coming. He leaned forward in his chair with his head under the table and treated us to the sound of retching and little smacklets of undigested rib bites hitting the floor of the courtyard. Obviously we wanted to leave immediately, but we stayed so as to not attract attention to the mess he was making. He was our friend and he was temporarily down. He had his head under the table for a minute. When the sound of the vomiting stopped, it was replaced by a sound even more awful. A moaning sound, but not a moaning. Or a muffled voice but not really muffled. It sounded like Dan was talking with his hand over his mouth, but he wasn't.

"Dan, you okay?"

"aaanhaaaanhaanha"

"Dan, you alright?"

"aahnaaahnaaa"

"Dan, sit back up. People are watching."

Dan sat up. When he sat up he looked around at all of us with his mouth wide open like you do at the dentist's. It was wider than just open. It was like double-open. I thought he was maybe laughing.

"Dan, what are you doing? Shut your mouth."

"aaaaahnaa" Dan pointed to his jaw.

"Oh shit."

There was a tremendous boom of laughter.

While Dan was under the table, the vomiting became so violent that it forced his mouth open and it got stuck. His jaw was locked into the wide-as-fuck-open position and there was no budging it. It looked more open than you think mouths are ever supposed to get, and it looked incredibly painful. He didn't say it was painful. Dan could no longer speak, only moan. You need to be able to close your mouth or get it somewhere near closed in order to form words with your lips. You need to be able to touch your tongue to the back of your teeth or the roof of your mouth because that's where language is. Besides it being pretty funny, the sound Dan made when trying to speak was unpleasant, disquieting, and terrible and I'm pretty sure everyone wanted to get away from it because it had the potential of giving us all a bad night. I'm not sure where you are right now while you're reading this or if you are in the position to do this without embarrassing yourself, but when you get a chance, open your mouth as wide as you can and the try to say in a normal volume speaking voice, "O how life is strange and changeful." Try it. Sounds fucked up, right? It sounds like something is seriously wrong with you, right?

By this point, we are all starting to feel our cookies. Dan was feeling it as well. He was sitting up in his chair now and his eyes were rolling back in his head and he kept trying to talk. But it wasn't talk. It sounded awful, like that sound you just made when you tried to say, "O how life is strange and change-ful," with your mouth all jacked open like a palsy. It was not a conducive soundtrack for a night meant for pleasure and nice things.

"You have to go to the hospital."

Dan shook his head.

"We should call an ambulance."

Dan shook his head and his eyes rolled around and even though his mouth was open wide enough for me to put my fucking head in there, I could still recognize a smile on his face. The giant circle would widen when he smiled. It looked like his face was going to tear open at the corners of his mouth.

"Okay then. Fuck it. He doesn't want to go. Let's just go to another bar," somebody (not me) said.

We left the courtyard bar walking in a small pack down Decatur and Dan kept trying to say things. He was rubbing his hands all over his body and hanging his head back as he walked and he kept making those terrible sounds. It started to look and sound vaguely sexual (in a totally scary, creepy way) and it was becoming increasingly annoying. We walked into the next bar: four normal looking college students with their insane-looking friend whose mouth was jacked open all the way like he was really amazed at the bar we had just walked into. Everyone was staring at Dan. Dan was nodding his head to the music like nothing was wrong. He put quarters in the pool table and went around the bar asking people if they wanted to shoot a game. But he couldn't ask them anything. He just walked up to them and made that horrible sound with his mouth wide open and it probably looked like to them that he was trying to bite them. No one wanted to shoot. Dan refused to leave or go to the hospital. At one point he borrowed a pen and grabbed a napkin from the bar and wrote: *I feel great. I don't care about my face.* As proud as I was of him for that winning fuck-all attitude, the sound was just too much for me and I didn't understand why he kept trying to talk when no one could understand him. My buzz was pretty much killed so I went home.

The next morning Dan showed up at my place. He said he stayed out last night for another hour or so. At one point he wanted to smoke some pot to help kick in the roll a bit but he couldn't hit a bowl or a joint because he couldn't get his lips around it. Instead, they stopped by someone's house who had a bong and he had to stick the entire top of the bong inside his mouth and behind his teeth to get a hit. I asked him why he didn't just have someone blow smoke into his mouth. He hadn't thought of that. He said when he woke up that morning his jaw was still locked open. (Did I mention that Dan rode a scooter?) He said he rode his scooter to the hospital with his mouth still like that. He said he freaked out a lot of drivers and he also ate lots of things from the air like bugs. At the hospital, the doctors gave him a shot in the jaw and closed it for him. As soon as he got home from the hospital, it popped open again. He had to ride his scooter back to the hospital with his mouth still jacked wide open and have them redo it. The doctors wrapped a bandage around his head so it wouldn't happen again.

10

A Checklist For Single People

Stephanie Georgopolus

1. Compare your ex to someone new and feel relieved.

2. Compare your ex to someone new and feel regret.

3. Go on a terrible date that convinces you that you'll be alone forever.

4. Go on a series of promising dates and tell your friends "this might be it."

5. Let the holidays serve as a reminder of the last time you had someone to spend them with.

6. Spend the night drinking and dancing and kissing; walk home at 6 a.m. and feel content to be alone with the sunrise.

7. Listen to love songs that remind you of no one; feel indifferent about feeling indifferent.

8. Listen to songs that remind you of the past and cry in the fetal position.

9. Be enough for yourself.

10. Do the things your past relationships discouraged; be the person your past relationships suppressed.

11. Feel woefully behind and kind of nervous every time a friend gets engaged.

12. Forget how hard it is to watch your relationship dissolve when doling out advice.

13. Get defensive when your relationship non-status becomes a topic of conversation at Thanksgiving.

14. Sleep diagonal because you can.

15. Feel high after a successful first date.

16. Wonder if you can fall in love with someone despite the absence of an initial spark.

17. Make out with someone for no reason other than you're both single and attractive.

18. Date people who are completely wrong for you because you clearly don't know who's right for you.

19. Get drunk and mentally forgive people your sober mind can't absolve.

20. Discover one day that you've stopped looking and started living; let that make you smile.

11

A Guide To Vague Relationships

Megan Boyle

A vague relationship basically feels like a real relationship, only it's harder to tell when it's okay to cuddle.

Vague relationships can last anywhere from 0 to 8 years, but are usually just a few months long.

You can have a vague relationship with your co-worker, your friend, your friend's brother, your brother's friend, your co-worker's brother, your brother's co-worker, your friend's brother's co-worker, or your brother's co-worker's friend – but not your brother.

Vague relationships are vague because their boundaries are never discussed.

Their boundaries are never discussed because one participant thinks that makes things more "exciting."

More "exciting" means it's acceptable to pursue other relationships and sleep with other people.

Sleeping with other people is fun because sex is like TV.

Sex is like TV because it is visually stimulating and mentally engaging for short periods of time.

Vague relationships have lots of sex, but no commercials.

Recommended to have on hand at all times

Full-length mirror. This is the most effective and thorough tool for confirming your attractiveness.

Birth control. This can be in the form of pills, condoms, or good intentions.

A pet. Pets are reliable sources of affection. Generally speaking, the larger the pet is, the more affectionate it will be (excluding horses).

- *Average lifespan of a goldfish:* 0-18 months
- *Average lifespan of a hamster:* 1-3 years

How to Enter a Vague Relationship

Get introduced to an attractive friend of a friend, co-worker, brother of a friend, etc. Anticipate having a boring conversation. Feel surprised when the conversation turns out to be interesting. Make each other laugh.

Spend enough time talking to discover you have enough things in common to have sex that night. See each other once a week, then a few times a week. Make sure he calls you more than you call him.

An Important Equation

$$[(\text{Sex})+(\text{every time you see each other})]$$
$$* [(\text{Genuine Interest})/(\text{uncertainty})]$$

$$\rule{4cm}{1pt}$$

$$\text{Time} - \text{discussion}(\text{``Official Commitment''})$$

F.A.Q. #1:

Q: "Should I ask about his ex-girlfriends?"

A: No. It is important to avoid the word "girlfriend."

Sample Introductions to Friends

- "This is my co-worker, Frank."
- "This is Amy, my friend."
- "My co-worker, Amy."
- "I met Frank at work."
- "Frank, my friend. We met at work."
- "Amy knew my brother from high school, actually."
- "Oh, my brother introduced us. He and Frank work together."

Nice Thing to Overhear

"I've actually never had as much fun with a girl as I do with Amy."

Four Steps to a Wild Thursday Night

1. Text him, "I'm bored, want to come grocery shopping?"
2. Wait a few hours before concluding that he probably read "grocery shopping" and thought "sweatpants" and possibly "marriage," which is why he hasn't responded.
3. Swallow one Xanax bar and walk to Whole Foods.
4. Tomorrow morning find three different kinds of lettuce and organic "Tea Tree Tingle" shower gel in your refrigerator.

Psychology lesson

A hamster is the subject of an experiment about reinforcement. When the hamster is hungry, it can press a button to receive a food pellet. If the hamster is rewarded a food pellet every time it presses the button, it will know to press the button when it is hungry. If the hamster is never rewarded, it will feel hungry all of the time and learn that the button is not associated with food pellets. If a food pellet is only sometimes rewarded to the hamster, it will press the button all of the time, never sure of when its hunger will end.

- *Average lifespan of a cat:* 12-15 years
- *Average lifespan of a horse:* 25-30 years

F.A.Q. #2:

Q: "Is it okay to daydream about camping together and maybe getting trapped in a cave and needing to subsist on crickets and dirt until we find this really pretty, bio-luminescent 'cave pool' filled with good-tasting fish and the water is warm enough to swim in and I accidentally get pregnant and when he delivers my baby he has the same look on his face as Clive Owen in *Children of Men* when he delivers the baby?"

A: No.

Bad Thing to Overhear

"No, I'm not seeing anyone."

Dinner Date

If you do have to break down and have a conversation with him about this "thing it is that you're doing," know that you have approached the end of your vague relationship, because you will be attempting to define it. A good place to have this conversation is your living room. A bad place to have this conversation is the parking lot outside of P.F. Chang's, before you've even sat down to dinner. When you get out of the car, the least appropriate-seeming thing to see is a faux-marble, grimacing Chinese lion.

Your Solo Cirque du Soleil Act

Try to hold yourself from behind

- *Average lifespan of a human:* **80 years**

Petsmart

This is a convenient and affordable one-stop shop for all of your small pet's needs, but try to avoid walking near the "Adopt a Cat" room with floor to ceiling glass. This room should especially be avoided when there are no other people around, so it's easy to stare at the neon stickers that advertise, "I'm a Snuggler!" and "Loves to Play!" Try not to think about the one fluorescent light that stays on all night after the employees go home.

F.A.Q. #3

Q: "Is the meaning of life to get excited about someone, genuinely feel interested in what he says, try to make him feel interested in what you say, make your bodies touch a lot, then 'mess up' somehow, have a long discussion where you 'talk about a lot' but don't actually talk about anything although you tell yourselves you've reached some kind of 'resolution,' see him less at parties, write things to him and regret it, cycle through desire and hatred towards him but sort of feel unjustified for feeling anything towards him at all, try to get interested in other things or people, have long stretches of time of just sitting in your bed, looking out the window and wondering how it got to be so late, crave physical contact, crave someone validating your existence by showing interest in you, maybe get drunk by yourself a few nights and fall asleep in the bathtub, wake up, and go to work the next day?"

12

The Definition of Love

Ryan O'Connell

You can stop taking quizzes in *Cosmo*. Here's what love really is.

Love is still wanting to hold someone after you climax. After the initial euphoria from the orgasm wears off, you're replaced with a sense of calm rather than a panic. You don't want to search for your clothes, scramble to find your keys and figure out the best way to tell them, "See ya later forever!" You're fine with chilling out in bed with the person and maybe ordering pad thai later.

Love is unattractive. It can expose our worst traits: Jealousy, irrational fears, heated anger; the gang's all here! While it can bring out compassion and tenderness, it can also make you behave like the ugliest version of yourself. That can be okay for a little while, but love with real longevity should be like a Xanax rather than an Adderall.

Love is not afraid to be schmaltzy. There's a reason why the most popular love songs are so lyrically simple. You can drown it in metaphors all you want but love usually boils down to, "You make me so happy. I want to hold your hand. I just want u 2 be mine 4ever!" You can be a 50-year-old linguistics professor at Columbia University and still find something to relate to in a Mariah Carey ballad if you're in love because the feelings are so universal. It's humbling, isn't it? No matter who you are or what your background is, love can reduce you to Mariah Carey mush.

Love is an all-consuming drug. It gives us these natural highs we've only read about in books or heard in songs. It's addictive. It's what keeps us going to bars, drinking glasses of wine, going to that stupid house party in Bushwick; it's all for the possibility of finding love. In the wrong hands, love can be dangerous and scary. If someone lacks a healthy foundation, love can kill. All of these crimes you read about in the newspapers are usually linked to passionate love. "I did it because I loved them just...too much."

Love is not what our parents had. In high school, you never wanted to think about your mother and father having once slept with people in the backseat of cars and feeling warm and happy. That would make it feel less special and young. It would make love have less to do with you when, EXCUSE ME, it has EVERYTHING to do with you.

Love is getting drunk with your significant other at a party and taking a cab home with your bodies intertwined. You feel safest in these moments, the most secure. Entering a social gathering with someone who loves you is the biggest security blanket. People leave the party as a parade of droopy expressions and sad cocktail dresses. But not you. "Sorry guys, I'm in love! I'm taking a car!"

Love is fucking stupid. Love is fucking smart. Love is about betraying yourself, of compromising your ideals for someone else's approval. That's actually the bad kind of love, but I guess it all blurs together when you're young or when you're old or when you don't love yourself.

Love is your significant other telling you about their favorite album and then making a point to fall in love with it on your own. Love is wondering why your better half loves certain things. You think you can find remnants of them in their favorite films, books and songs, but you usually can't.

Love is finding yourself feeling protective over someone else's well-being Love is being incensed with rage when someone or something has done your lover wrong.

Love is wanting your partner to cum. And if they can't, just say, "That's okay. I'm enjoying this." It might be bullshit, but they'll be orgasming in the next five minutes. Trust me.

Love isn't always marriage. Marriage is spending $60,000 so everyone can know that someone loves you. You know what's certainly not love? Debt. In some cases, love can be divorce.

Love is a back massage, a mindfuck, a hard cock, a pair of perfect breasts, of feeling unashamed about the cellulite on your body. Love is someone giving a shit about you enough to argue. Love is not passive. Love is "Don't fucking touch me right now." Love is "Who the FUCK were you talking to?" Love is sometimes hating yourself for a second. Love is hate. Period. Indifference is the real killer of love and the true antithesis.

When love leaves you, you should be lying on your bathroom floor with no resolve. You're smoking cigarettes in the bathtub and crying about everything bad that's ever happened.

Love is someone seeing the beauty in you and wanting to bask in it every day all day. Love is not guaranteed. We are not owed love. That's why when we get it, we know how lucky we are and hold on to it for dear life.

So, yeah. That's what love is. Anyone know where to get some?

13

A Checklist For Your Mid 20s

Brandon Scott Gorrell

1. Watch your group of friends change — some marry and fade, best friends unexpectedly become strange, new acquaintances suddenly offer perspectives which are simultaneously impossible to ignore, intriguing, unrealistic, exciting, and awareness-of-self inducing.

2. Realize your perception of people you meet on the internet has gone from 'exciting/ forbidden' (age 10-13) to 'subversive guilty pleasure' (age 14-21) to 'can't discern if culturally acceptable' (age 22-23) to 'can't discern if accurately reflects reality' (age 24-??).

3. Realize your idea of friendship is reworking itself, seemingly beyond your control — individuals with certain characteristics who, at age 18, would have not met your standards suddenly find themselves in your favor, perhaps the consequence of convenience, compromise, or a softening of ideals.

4. Have a battle with drinking — are you sophisticated, a drunk, affluent, depressed, bored, psycho, killing time, having fun, are you too old for this? Is this a spiral? Is a half-bottle of wine acceptable? Is an entire bottle of wine acceptable? Is even getting drunk acceptable? I blacked out the other night, fuck.

5. Become genuinely compelled by high culture food, e.g., sushi, kale, organic, local, fusion, sweet potato fries, Bloody Marys, salmon, brunch, tartar, -ianisms; feel aware/ suspicious/ anxious about your newly acquired interest; perceive what you will later come to know as "first world guilt."

6. Realize resolution of first world guilt has become a major unconscious agenda; the agenda is vague and unanswerable to an extent — the fact may be simply that you are, in a completely egregious way, not currently a person starving in a third world country.

7. Struggle with the tenets of individualism; earnestly believe, contradictorily, the entitled stance that you're special and that your unique contribution to the world will pay off, as well as the stance that you're not at all special and that the idea of having a unique contribution to offer is a cliché and simply not a universal given, but instead a common, scrutable perception of reality.

8. Ask yourself how it's even possible to change anything; feel nervous about the inherent apathy embedded within the latter question — and thus embedded in your worldview and so feel doomed to some sort of facist corporate apocalyptic future scenario as well as a personal mediocrity that ultimately seems bleak and irredeemable.

9. Have regular flashbacks of your childhood, which revolved around figuring out how to work a lighter, playing hockey on rollerblades in someone's cul-de-sac, and feeling like the whole neighborhood felt you their son or daughter; remember the lake, remember the plastic smell of toys, remember the smell of your best friend's basement, remember blowing out a Nintendo cartridge, remember the asphalt, the first hand-hold.

10. Recall the present; realize, confusingly, that it is what it is; concurrently understand that you've accepted the passing of childhood and decided that childhood-related nostalgia is something to be enjoyed but ultimately discarded — understand both concepts as unnecessary albeit meaningful and sigh-inducing; feel unsure, feel capable, feel okay, feel career-minded, still know your childhood address, feel afraid, feel drunk, feel annoyed, remember your back yards, remember the intrigue of your parents' bedroom, feel concerned about tomorrow, feel invested in your boyfriend's outfit, feel hurt she still talks to her ex, feel confident, remember the sound of the bell that called you in from recess, feel doomed, feel free.

14

The 3 Times I Took Ambien

Karyn Spencer

The first time I took Ambien, I worked for an actor and our schedule was bananas. When you're filming a movie, you have to shoot all night to finish one outdoor nighttime scene. We'd work three or four days from 6pm-6am and then the next couple of days we'd go back to shooting during the day. We bounced back and forth from days to nights like that every week and big surprise, my body did not like it.

After my first few weeks of this, I was so screwed up that I couldn't fall asleep during the time allotted for sleep. My brain turned to cheese and I constantly felt like I was going to burst into tears.

The on-set doctor heard me complaining and sent me home with a bag of Ambien samples. What she failed to tell me was to read the directions. Maybe she thought that was obvious? Please. I assemble IKEA furniture on the fly. I don't seek advice from enclosed literature.

Well! Turns out the most important thing about Ambien is

that once you take it, you should *immediately get in bed, turn the lights off, and close your eyes.*

I can't stress this enough. If you don't do that, parts of your brain turn off, but your body keeps functioning. Literally, the lights are on but no one's home.

I swallowed the pill, and thinking I should chillax until it made me sleepy, went downstairs and started watching TV. Oprah was on the DVR. *Hey, I like Oprah. Oh, sweet! James Frey is on!*

Then I woke up in a sand trap on a golf course in my pajamas.

There was a message on my phone from my dude that said "I'm forwarding you the voice mail you left me last night. Please review and explain".

Baaby. I dun wan Operah to lose her Oprahness. But whaa is she doin to my James Frey? She was soo. Wrong. He was hurtin. She was hurtin. So much pain. Pain pain pain pain. T Pain. He's a rapper. It's a raaaap. So yeah, what a show. What. A. Show. Shit show. Pile of Snow. Anywayyyyyyyyyy, wish you were here. You know how you get all sexy and I pretend like I dun likeit? Well I do. And if you were here. Maaan. OK baaby gonna go play some golf now luuuuuuuuuv you.

The second time I took Ambien, I decided to stay in my room and finish up a few emails before I hit the hay.

The next morning my boss looked at me funny and said, "Um, so that was a really nice email you sent, thanks."

I ran to my sent folder and found this:

Hey you! Whassup! I just want you to know that I am really proud of you. You are doing a good job. You don't ever complain. You really set a great example. I like you. Keep spreadin all your sunshine around! Love, Karyn

I SENT THAT TO MY BOSS.

The third time I took Ambien, apparently because idiots do things in threes, I was flying in a private plane to Europe. Sometimes I roll fancy like that.

There was a lot of work to be done when I landed, so I wanted to get a solid ten hours of sleep on the flight. I thought that's what I did. Then I downloaded my travel pictures, and found thirty shots of myself from very odd angles in the plane's bathroom that I have absolutely no memory of taking. There was a sleep mask resting on the top of my head that failed to keep me blacked out. And while my eyes were vacant and trance-like, my odd open-mouthed expression of surprise freaks me out the most. Guess I was super excited that Ambien just can't keep me down.

15

Meet Me Offline

Stephanie Georgopulos

Meet me offline tonight, 'cause a 73 x 73 thumbnail isn't enough *you*. I want you in the highest resolution, in four dimensions, the only way I know how to look at something beautiful. You weren't made for the screen you know, and neither was the broken skin where you cut yourself shaving and the almost-invisible hairs that paint the corners of your upper lip and that one crooked eyelash that bends at a 45-degree angle. Who was foolish enough to think they could squeeze everything noteworthy about you into an avatar? You're too pretty for pixels.

Put up an away message and let's go away, somewhere we can power down and still feel electric, somewhere that doesn't need password protecting. Let's lose ourselves and find ourselves in a place with no Yelp reviews, no Google results, no Foursquare check-ins. The distance between your eyes and mine is uncharted territory, that's a good place to start. Let's look there first.

Tonight, I want to push all of your buttons except the one that says Like. I want to eat too slowly and argue over Tim Burton's best film and take your mother's side; I want you to look at me like you want to strangle me or kiss me or both and maybe then I'll undo a couple of your buttons or my buttons and how's that for a notification? I want to be the one to alert you.

Sign off and log out and shut down so we can meet up and go out and get high on fingers touching fingers and tongues pressing tongues instead of fingers pressing buttons. What I want to give to you is too large to attach, what I want to give to you can't be uploaded or emailed or right-click-saved. Meet me so that we can remember how to connect without a router and a modem and a satellite, do it so that we don't forget.

Just unplug for a while, 'cause I can't download the space between your shoulder blades and I need your back in my hands to remember how bodies work. I want to relearn your skin with an open palm, not a single finger, you know what I mean? 'Cause what I mean is I want to touch you, not Poke you; I want to like you, not Like you; I want to love you, not Heart you. I want to live in a place void of scare quotes, of capitalized letters that inject semantics, a place void of tonal ambiguity. I want to live in a place where the space between your back exists, where it's wire-less and not wireless, a place where I can like you in lowercase. Let me like you.

16

Don't Wake Up Alone On A Saturday Morning

Ryan O'Connell

Your life is changing in small, important ways every day. The structure is no longer holding, no longer able to stay glued together, so certain things are having to leave you when you're asleep. They're so quiet, so considerate when they abandon you, that I bet you don't even notice.

They call this growing up, or something similar to it. You wake up on a Saturday morning and realize everything has become unrecognizable to you. The gauze has been lifted! When did this happen? Oh right, when you were sleeping. They came in at night and started to peel things away from you like an orange. They were careful not to cut the center, they were careful not to let any juice drip on the bedspread your mother bought for you. They wanted your life to look familiar to you, didn't want to shock you completely, so they kept some things intact. Some things, not everything. Guess what's gone? Wrong. Guess again.

You woke up on a Saturday and came to the sudden realization that you were all alone, that everything you had surrounded yourself with Monday through Friday, all the happy hours and all the business lunches and all those technological noises you drenched your earbuds in: it all added up to zero. You feel like a fool, don't you? You played the game like everyone asked you to and still managed get to this place of complete and utter loneliness and alienation. Where did you go wrong? Do you need to send another text message to someone? Do you need to pay another credit card off or have another Great Night Out? What can you do to feel more connected to the things around you?

On Friday night, everyone was right next to you. There was Olivia and Taylor and Ethan and Josh and Michael and Sarah, and they were all here by your side laughing and drinking and taking pictures. No one left till the morning and you went to bed just as the sun was hitting your eyes. When you woke up, it was three p.m. and already dark out. You found out that, while you were sleeping, Josh married Olivia and they moved to the country somewhere. Sarah went to grad school and had a baby in New Hampshire. She's gone. She wrote the last chapter of her book and she'll never be relevant to you again. You wonder what happened to Michael. Well, let's see. You loved Michael more than what was good for you and after sleeping with him for five years, it fell down like a game of cards. You don't have the right to speak to him anymore. You lost it when you lost him. Say good-bye to that. Ethan is living in Portland and makes annoying Facebook updates about his life as a mountain climber and Taylor became a heroin addict. Just kidding! She writes books about organic farming.

How did this all happen when you were sleeping? How did you manage to sleep through all of these events? You were asleep and now you're awake but it's too late. Everyone else already went to bed and now you're just alone and awake on a Saturday morning and that's it. This is it. Never fall asleep again.

17

You'll Never Be Able To Pull Yourself Together

Leigh Alexander

At some point, preferably in the evening when the desolation of night presses down on you — cars and the implacable noises of distant strangers, leftover smells of other people's meals, the artificial tide of faraway cars ebbing and sighing — you will look around your place or residence and realize, dimly, that you do not feel you have your shit together.

You will deduce this from a largely arbitrary assemblage of features. You have a coffee table on which the receipts touch the napkins, and you wonder why you put them there instead of throwing them away. Maybe that makes you think about how you put magazines on your bedroom dresser for decoration, or because you intended to read them or because they represent your interests and they're still there, even though they're ambassadors of a month beginning with 'M' and it's now September.

Perhaps on the inside of your coat closet door or in some other obscure location you have a calendar that says a month beginning with 'M.' It's September. You know because you are behind on something: Your deadline, your New Year's resolution, your friend or relative's birthday, things you were supposed to have had done by this point in September.

Your awareness of all your loose ends unravels subtly like smoke curling in the air (you were supposed to quit smoking several times over the past several years) until its tendrils touch everything — your disarranged shelves, your un-upholstered furniture, your impersonal, unpainted living room walls. It snakes over your floorboards (swept, but unwashed) into your bedroom and over your unmade bed, it notices the dust that has settled inside the bellies of your decorative candles, long-unlit.

There are the toys that you can still locate — figurines, kitsch, gag gifts, inappropriate fixtures for an adult life. Mentally inventory the child-like baskets where you keep your discount shoes, or the sloppy tray of your discount cosmetics, your drugstore toilette, whatever subtle edges of frayed disorder threaten to expose you as someone who does not have his or her shit together.

You think about your one strange habit; everybody has one strange habit. Perhaps it is that you are loath to switch from your beloved, well-worn toothbrush to a brand new, rubber-bristled and neon-studded alien of an unfamiliar thing, and so you procrastinate the transition until you feel unreasonable. Or maybe it's how you never, never put anything in a frame. Or it's how you leave in your apartment mail box your junk letters, or the bills you don't want to pay, or the things that say RESIDENT. Because you don't really want to deal with something so small as a sheaf of meaningless envelopes, or because an empty mailbox looks starkly dysfunctional, unsettling. The dishes you washed remain in the rack because, to be honest, you just don't use them that much. You eat out a lot; the wrapped packages, the containers in your fridge you will never touch, are for show. You do not know how old they are.

You have X-Amount of debt. You are adept at putting it out of your head, but at times like this, when you're thinking about something extreme, the X-Amount looms like a stopper in your sluice, an insurmountable clog. I know someone who is still afraid to flush the toilet in the middle of the night, scathed by a childhood experience of being scolded for being awake when she ought not to've been. I have never asked her if she thinks of her debt and her unwept midnight basin at the same time, in the same terms.

You make a list of things you should stop doing, that include drinking so much (alcohol, coffee), or going on dates with the sort of people that require you to nod politely, mentally checked out, your knuckles white and fingertips electric against the urge to reach for your phone and idly read your Twitter feed while they are talking. You should work out. Maybe you should make an Excel spreadsheet about your goals, and your goals are do more this and do less that. They are "write a book" or something that makes you feel reprehensible (you are considering mantra; you feel stupid).

You go to events featuring people who have written books and all most of them do is levy theatrical complaints about how hard it is to make money and get famous, and how they get writer's block or something absurd.

Maybe they just don't have their shit together. But, I mean, if you are a writer or an artist or an actor or something like that, are you really supposed to have your shit together? And then supposing you are a chef or an aspiring small business owner or nursing student or something like that, you can always tell yourself you're in a competitive field with various bottlenecks unique to your chosen occupation, and that nothing is ever a straight line from point A to point B, and sometimes wanting things is not enough and all kinds of obstacles arise to dissuade you such as finances, life issues, [something else], whatever, and you are at a normal point on some imagined progression line.

Become temporarily overwhelmed by the number of variables you must act upon in order to effect change in your life sufficient enough that you would feel that you have your shit together. As you attempt to count them all up, become disoriented.

Visualize your ultimate destination as a polished, sterile location with a polished, sterile partner and you are polished and sterile.

Ultimately, you would look around your fiberglass pod of a futuristic Success Destination and figure that your sluices probably could be siphoned better or that you wish you could afford more frequent visits to the person who lifts your browline up expertly with a little suture twisted like a key in a lock, smoothing and tightening. Maybe you would work someplace really impressive but then you get home and everyone on the internet is complaining about the interface redesign measures you worked for several months to implement and you look at your robot maid and your Pod-Children and the fact that there is a single, aberrant, unopened envelope on your Culinary Module. From somewhere in your house an Interloping Bacteria Detector chimes in dissatisfaction and you feel that you do not have your shit together.

On the face of the digital newspaper device to which you subscribe in your theoretical future, a person with an even better body than yours has been abandoned by his or her significant other, even though he or she has someone to handle his or her accounting.

Your own body is silently waging a war of manifold fronts on the microscopic level against entropy. You are shuttling dead cells through your system inefficiently. You are oxidizing and platelets are becoming stuck. Somewhere on the planet's face an insect pushes tiny granules uphill. The granules tumble, its mandibles move, it pushes them uphill again. Nobody has their shit together. You never will.

18

How To Be A 20-Something

Ryan O'Connell

Be really attractive. Your acne is gone, your face has matured without having wrinkles and everything on your body is lifted naturally. Eat bagels seven days a week, binge-drink and do drugs: you'll still look like a babe. When you turn thirty, it'll become a different story but that's, like, not for a really long time.

Reestablish a relationship with your parents. You don't live with them anymore (hopefully) so start to appreciate them as human beings with thoughts, flaws and feelings rather than soulless life ruiners who won't let you borrow their car.

Go from eating delicious food at your parents' house to eating Ragu tomato sauce over Barilla noodles. Develop an eating disorder to save money.

Move into an apartment on the corner of Overpriced and Dangerous. Sleep on a bare mattress with an Ikea comforter. Your mother talks to you about buying a top sheet and a duvet cover but feel like you're not mature enough to own something called "duvet."

"Date people who you know you'll never be able to love."

Read the *New York Times* piece, "What Is It About 20-Somethings?" Feel exposed and humiliated. Share it on your Facebook with the caption: "Um…." Your friends will comment "Too real" and that will be the end of that.

Work at a coffee shop but feel hopeful about your career in advertising, writing, whatever. Remember that you're young and that the world is your oyster. Everything is possible, you still have so much to see and hear. You went to a good school and did good things. Figure if you're not going to be successful, who the hell is?

Date people who you know you'll never be able to love. See someone for three months for no other reason than because it's winter and you want to keep warm by holding another body. Date a Republican just so you can say you dated a Republican.

Eventually all these nobodies will make you crave a somebody. Have a real relationship with someone. Go on vacations together, exchange house keys, cry in their arms after a demoralizing day at work. Think about marrying them and maybe even get engaged. Regardless of the outcome, feel proud of yourself for being able to love someone in a healthy way.

Start your twenties with a lot of friends and leave with a few good ones. What happened? People faded away into their careers and relationships. Fights were had and never resolved. Shit happens.

Think of yourself at twenty and hanging out with people who didn't mean a thing to you. Think about writing papers, about being promiscuous, about trying new things. Think of yourself now and your face looking different and your body feeling different and how everything is just different.

Form the habits that will stick with you forever. Drink your coffee with two sugars and skim milk every morning. Buy a magazine every Friday. Enjoy spending money on candles, smoke pot on Saturdays, watch the television before bed.

Move into a bigger apartment on the corner of Mature and Gentrification and finally buy a duvet cover. Limit your drug-use. If you find yourself unable to do so, start to wonder if you have a problem.

Have your parents come to your place for Christmas. Set the table, make the ham, wear a sophisticated outfit, This will all mean so much at the time.

Think about having children when you stop acting like a child. This may not ever happen.

Maybe this is assuming too much. Maybe this is generalizing. Maybe society uses age as an unrealistic marker for growth. Maybe. Still feel the anxiety on your 30th birthday and think to yourself, "Oh shit, I'm no longer a 20-something."

Thought Catalog, it's a website.

www.thoughtcatalog.com

Social

facebook.com/thoughtcatalog
twitter.com/thoughtcatalog
tumblr.com/thoughtcatalog
instagram.com/thoughtcatalog

Corporate

www.thought.is

20870541R00056

Printed in Great Britain
by Amazon